1 MONTH OF
FREE
READING

at
www.ForgottenBooks.com

By purchasing this book you are eligible for one month membership to ForgottenBooks.com, giving you unlimited access to our entire collection of over 1,000,000 titles via our web site and mobile apps.

To claim your free month visit:
www.forgottenbooks.com/free889258

ISBN 978-0-265-78683-3
PIBN 10889258

Louisiana
Conservationist
CONTENTS

Pg. 4

Pg. 23

Pg. 25

Front Cover The Big Catch
By Doug Stamm

Back Cover Bullfrog
By Gary Kramer

Published by the Department of Wildlife and Fisheries in the interest of conservation of Louisiana natural resources.

Quality Angling at Chicot Lake

BY CHRIS BERZAS

The current lake record stands at 13.53 pounds. The first 15 pound black bass taken by hook and line out of Chicot and weighed at official scales will earn the fortunate angler some $5,000.

In the land of the Mamou Two-Step, the melodies of the accordion and fiddle give way to an Evangeline Parish secret nestled just north of the city of Ville Platte, home of the endeared Pig Stand and classic Floyd's Record Shop.

Within the very heart of beautiful Chicot State Park, a 1,642 acre cypress-studded reservoir suddenly appears and teases ardent anglers away from the indigenous aromas of boudin, cracklins, tasso and crawfish etouffee.

One could certainly say that Chicot Lake plays its own tune in these parts, one that has anglers from throughout the state jigging

energetically. The rhythm just has to be about fishing, and it's a double-digit tune for bass, slab-sided sac-a-lait and gargantuan bull bream.

"There's no doubt we have a real quality fishery here," claimed Jody David, Inland Fisheries Biologist with the Louisiana Department of Wildlife and Fisheries (LDWF). "We've seen Chicot Lake really come around, especially with bass, with three trophy lunkers over 13 pounds taken in 1995. The current lake record stands at 13.53 pounds taken in 1995 by John Darbonne of Eunice.

"In 1996 we had one fish over 11 pounds, as well as several seven to 10 pound fish," added the biologist. "So far in 1997, we have had an 11.2 pounder, three over 10, and others ranging from seven to nine pounds."

What's the secret?

For one thing, Chicot Lake is one of only a few waterbodies in Louisiana specially designated by LDWF as a Quality Lake. Besides being stocked with more than a million Florida bass fingerlings since 1987, the bass management program here currently dictates a daily limit of eight fish including a slot limit of 14-17 inches.

In other words, all bass from 14 to 17 inches long must be released immediately, and only four fish over 17 inches may be kept in the daily creel of eight.

"In terms of genetics, our electro-fishing studies indicate the presence of the Florida strain in about 50 percent of the fish sampled," raved David. "That's a great indication that the lunker trait is taking root, and we hope for even larger fish in the future. I'm now expecting a few more 13 pounders in 1997, as well as a 15 pound fish or better."

What's very interesting about the 1997 trophies has to do with the fact that these beauties have shown up despite the hydrilla control drawdown last fall and winter. Anglers were seriously concerned prior to the drawdown that lowered water levels would have a disastrous consequence in terms of catch rate.

Well that hasn't happened at Chicot. The months of January and February produced some hefty stringers.

"Based on what I've seen this past spring, we were pleasantly surprised with quality bass," said Skip Kovach of Lafayette, a 38-year old insurance executive and avid Chicot Lake bass angler. "In January and February, it was common to catch 12 to 15 bass per day with two to five fish in the five to seven pound range.

"And I look for May and June to consistently produce good fish," added Kovach. "They may not be in the order of the double-digit fish taken during the spawn, but there will be many fish in the five- to eight- pound range."

Patterning quality bass is Kovach's passion, and he advises visiting anglers to search for duckweed at this time of the year. Throwing plastic, Louisiana Lightning magnum topwater frogs atop this vegetation can certainly result in some violent hooksets at this time of the year.

"I would advise anglers to visit the northern end, colloquially referred to as the Branch and Turtle Island Cove areas," stressed Kovach. "We found good spawning fish in the area and I do believe these fish will back off a little deeper after the spawn. If you can find submerged grass in four to six feet of water, I would also use plastic jerkbaits to entice them. As the day progresses, black Ring Rascal four-inch plastic worms with red metal flakes can produce some solid action in the same areas."

Kovach is indeed happy with the management success at Chicot Lake but personally feels that a Trophy Lake designation should be in its future.

"This is a relatively small waterbody and the fishing pressure here can get rather severe at times," noted Kovach. "I would hope that a 15-19 inch slot would be in the lake's future, with only one fish allowed to be harvested over the 19- inch mark.

"Harvest pressure would then be put on the smaller fish which are much safer to eat anyway with the amount of mercury contamination reportedly present in the larger fish," reasoned Kovach. "In this way, anglers will always have the opportunity to keep a trophy fish, and fish that are eaten will be safer for everyone."

At present, there is even a big-bass award program in force at Chicot Lake. The first 15 pound black bass taken out of Chicot will earn the fortunate angler some $5,000. In addition, $1,000 and $500 will be awarded respectively to the angler(s) reeling in the largest and second-largest black bass in each of the next three years. (First year: 12:01 a.m., June 30, 1996 - noon June 29, 1997; second year June 30, 1997 - June 29, 1998 and third year, June 30, 1998 - June 29, 1999).

All participants must have a valid Louisiana Office of State Parks (LOSP) receipt in their possession and must abide by all the rules and regulations. The black bass must also be certified according to the official Louisiana Outdoor Writers Association's (LOWA) fish

Electro-fishing studies indicate the presence of the Florida strain in about 50 percent of the bass sampled.

Photo by Chris Berzas

records rules and each fish must be taken by hook and line.

Also, each fish must be weighed at the official, certified scales provided at the Manager's Office at Chicot State Park by a certified and authorized representative of the LOSP. Until a LDWF fisheries biologist can be summoned, the fish can be placed in a "Living Stream" tank located at the old boat dock.

Both the LOSP and the LDWF recommend, but do not mandate, that the fish be released alive back into Chicot Lake. The LOSP will provide replica mounts free-of-charge of any of the large bass entered into the "catch-n-release" portion of the program. The only cost incurred is the $20 fee required with the LOWA application form.

But, enough said about bass fishing. Chicot Lake is also noted for some quality crappie angling as well. Colloquially referred to here as "white perch" and "sac-a-lait", these speckled beauties are sought after avidly by numerous anglers.

"Prior to the drawdown, we were catching quality fish in good numbers," said noted Chicot Lake angler Glynn Lavergne of Savoy. "However, now I expect quality sac-a-lait, but probably not in the numbers seen prior to the draw-down. That's based on my experiences fishing after the previous draw-down.

"In May and June I would fish the edges of grass beds or floating plants," recommends the angler. "Sure, you may find some good fish jigging vertically within structure, but I'd also cast to these fish that work the edges as well."

Lavergne casts 1/32-ounce Louisiana Lightning tube jigs in the following color combinations: yellow/white, black/chartreuse and orange/white. These tubes are worked with 8 ft. flyrods equipped with ultralight spincast reels spooled with six pound-test monofilament.

Another unique method employed by Lavergne has to do with the action of the jighead. Lavergne attaches the head of the jig with a tiny loop which allows the jig more freedom of movement. He feels that this is an important factor to the pressured fish at Chicot.

Lavergne insists that anglers should try these sac-a-lait techniques in the Branch Area and areas around the North Landing. Move south as the waters clear, where some phenomenal sac-a-lait in the 2 1/2- pound range can be taken.

As for bream, there is no argument that Chicot Lake traditionally delivers gargantuan bulls to anglers in May and June. The coves on the northwestern side are popular and bedding fish can be found in these areas on points near the Branch and Conservation Lodge areas. Crickets and worms are the most popular offerings, cast to these fish with ultralight equipment.

In the last year, two walk-on 400-foot piers were constructed near the North and South landings respectively. Structure in the form of Christmas trees was also placed along the edges of the pier on the northern end. In this way, panfish anglers without boats have access to some fine fishing opportunities on the lake.

At this time, park entrance is provided only at the northern entrance on Louisiana Highway 106. This is due to improvements under construction at the main southern entrance into the park. A new welcome station, widened roadway and additional parking will benefit Chicot in its future.

Chicot State Park consistently ranks as Louisiana's most visited state park, averaging over 200,000 visitors annually since 1994. The 6,400 acre site offers rental cabins and group camps as well as primitive and improved campsites, hiking trails, an olympic-sized swimming pool, group shelters and picnic areas.

For more information write or call: Chicot State Park, Route 3, Box 494, Ville Platte, LA 70586; phone: 318/363-2503; reservations: 318/363-2403. And good fishing! ◄

Two walk-on 400 foot piers (background of lower photograph) were constructed near the North and South landings. Now anglers without boats as well as those with boats can enjoy the fishing at Chicot Lake.

Photos by Chris Berzas

TRAGEDY TO TROPHIES

Photo by Holly Bergeret

State of the Art Hatchery Will Go for the Gold

BY HOLLY BERGERET

"How many fish can a fisherman fetch
If a fisherman can't find fish?"

In the aftermath of Hurricane Andrew, this tongue twister was a relevant question for many Louisiana fishermen. Not to mention conservationists, tourism officials and all others with a vested interest in the aquatic parlayer of food, fun and financial assets.

The 1992 storm lashed at the Louisiana coast and raged up the Atchafalaya Basin, causing fish kills estimated at 200 million fish. The largemouth bass population took a severe hit, depleting stocks in the Basin area by an estimated 4.5 million fish.

Catfish, bream, crappie and many other species were also casualties, their numbers decimated seemingly overnight by the harsh hand of Mother Nature. In the face of such ecological devastation, anglers wondered what would become of their beloved fish, particularly largemouth bass.

They needn't have worried. Atchafalaya's largemouth population has made a rapid comeback. The Department of Wildlife and Fisheries and private sportsmen and bass clubs undertook a massive restocking effort, and it wasn't long

This series of photograph shows the Booker Fowler Hatchery in its entirety. The top photograph is the hatchery office (foreground) and visitor center (background).

Photo by Holly Bergeret

The grounds include 55 one-acre rearing ponds, (middle) and 16 concrete raceways, shown in the bottom photograph.

Photo by Guy LaBranche

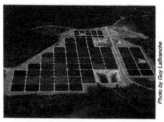

The complex is nestled between the 2,250-acre Indian Creek Reservoir and the rolling hills of lower Rapides Parish. Visitors will be impressed at the size of the hatchery and the invitingly designed blend of nature and modern architecture.

Photo by Guy LaBranche

before quality fish were being pulled out of the area and quantities began showing a significant rise. Across the bayou state, bass fishing is a tremendously popular and rewarding endeavor.

It's about to get better. Much better. Knowing that you can win the battle but lose the war, the Inland Fisheries Division has announced the long-anticipated grand opening of the newest weapon in their fisheries arsenal.

The $13 million, state of the art Booker Fowler Fish Hatchery will be unveiled to the public the first week of June. Adjacent to the Indian Creek Reservoir near Woodworth, it has been designated as the state's primary freshwater fish rearing facility.

Booker Fowler will be dedicated to raising no less than 85 million fish for stocking into disaster impacted and other state waters over the next 10 years. The facility will provide a nursery for Florida largemouth bass, blue, channel and flathead catfish, paddlefish, Gulf sturgeon and other species as the need arises.

There are high hopes for the ultramodern, 250-acre complex. The new technology will provide an opportunity for the state to address important environmental concerns.

LDWF biologist and Inland Fisheries Programs Manager, Arthur Williams, explains, "We've never had this capability before. It gives us a whole new concept in environmental possibilities. Beside the impact we will have stocking large numbers of Florida bass, it gives us the ability to do production of fish like Gulf sturgeon and Pallid sturgeon. The Gulf sturgeon is on the threatened list and the Pallid sturgeon is endangered. We now have the capacity to possibly bring them back from the brink of extinction."

Williams adds, "Fisheries is a highly technical program. We want people to know what we're doing with their money. Stocking fish is just a tool. Habitat management is the key."

The complex is nestled between 2,250 acre Indian Creek Reservoir and the rolling hills of lower Rapides Parish. Landscaping nurseries line the roadway off I-49 and exit 66 as you wind your way around the lushly wooded countryside and curves of Fish Hatchery Road toward your destination. Visitors will be impressed at the size of the hatchery and the invitingly designed blend of nature with modern architecture.

The Visitor Center is a modern public education facility. It stresses understanding the ecology, technology and responsibility involved in developing and preserving Louisiana's aquatic resources. Home to a 130-pound alligator snapping turtle, the center features wall displays and both fresh and saltwater aquariums. A 60-seat auditorium is provided to present educational videos and host classes and workshops.

The curious can also get a bird's eye view of the hatchery itself. Catwalks are provided to let guests observe the daily activities in the indoor wet lab, spawning and egg incubation rooms.

Raising and stocking potential trophies will be a careful blending of nature and high technology. And while America is striving to build a bridge to the 21st Century, the Booker Fowler hatchery will enable the Inland Fisheries Division to leap right into it.

The grounds are surrounded by 55 one-acre rearing ponds, 15 one-acre broodstock ponds, three smaller isolation ponds and 16 concrete raceways. The hatchery buildings house a spawning room with 40 fiberglass troughs, an egg incubation room and chemistry and diagnostic laboratories.

The compound also features a wet lab, feed preparation area, mechanical and life support rooms, office and conference space. Emergency power generators are available if the need arises. A kitchen area and men's and women's quarters are provided to enable 24-hour operation when necessary. Smaller buildings provide storage and maintenance areas. A private residence is also on the site for the hatchery supervisor.

"Intensive Culture" spawning techniques are being employed for the first time. Previously, fish were spawned naturally. Basically, they were put in a pond and allowed to spawn, and the eggs to hatch and grow. Now, nests are removed and transferred to indoor troughs to hatch. The fry are then seined and placed in rearing ponds.

These added steps will eliminate parental and carnivorous predation and maintain a uniform size and age. Survival is the second key. Previously a very high percentage of fry were lost shortly after after birth to preda-

Intensive culture spawning techniques are being employed for the first time. The top photograph shows hatchery staff separating male and female broodstock and placing it in raceways.

Photos by Holly Bergerel

Adult holding tanks (middle photograph) for sturgeon and paddlefish. Rearing troughs (bottom) where the eggs are hatched and fingerlings held until ready for stocking ponds.

These added steps will eliminate parental and carnivorous predation and maintain a uniform size and age. Survival is the key. Previously a very high percentage of fry were lost shortly after after birth to predation by the parents and older fingerlings.

tion by the parents and older fingerlings.

Unlike its predecessors, the facility has complete water quality control. Four wells and the nearby reservoir permit peak usage of 12,000 gallons of water per minute. It can be blended, disinfected, filtered, degassed, aerated and temperature-controlled as needed.

Wet and dry life support systems consist of water hardening equipment, chilling units, an ozone disinfecting unit, pure oxygen and a recirculating system. Polyethylene liners have been installed in all ponds. These will totally eliminate vegetation problems, diseases and parasitic organisms. In doing so, the liners provide the added benefit of preventing oxygen depleting organisms.

A modified catch basin has also been built into the drainage system. Designed by Inland Fisheries personnel, it allows easier harvesting and maximum drainage with less manpower.

To insure that a glitch somewhere in the system doesn't go undetected, a 16-point computerized monitoring system oversees the whole operation. If there happens to be a problem in oxygen levels or at the pumping station, the computer will alert staff to the problem.

Hatchery Program Manager Robert Gough aims to put a gleeful glimmer into the eyes of Louisiana's fishermen. "My ultimate goal is to produce the next world record largemouth bass for the United States in Louisiana," he says. "I really think that we have the potential to get there. We already have good quality parental stock. We've been stocking the Florida strain since 1986, but we didn't have quantity. Now we're going to have quantity."

Gough points out that the state record has been broken four times in the last five years alone. He believes our waters could capture the big one within the next five.

These lofty ambitions have been years in the making. They were molded in part by strategic planning, careful management and luck. By 1984, increased fishing pressure had reduced the native bass populations to numerous smaller fish, with a steadily declining number of larger ones.

Florida largemouth bass strains were introduced to Louisiana extensively beginning in 1986 to propagate a larger, faster growing bass to meet the public demand

and to provide a higher quality fishing experience. The Black Bass Management Plan followed in 1986, establishing trophy and quality lake designations and slot creel limits.

At the same time, LDWF realized it had a hatchery system with very little pond space. The three existing facilities, constructed between 1920-30, could not come close to meeting production needs of the management plan: 5,700,000 fingerlings a year to stock 57,000 acres of lakes.

In 1989 the Legislature allocated $1 million for a reconnaissance mission to find a suitable location to build a new hatchery. A site was selected, but disaster struck before funds could be appropriated for actual construction.

Andrew's 1992 excursion through south-central Louisiana, wiping out large quantities of fish in the Atchafalaya Basin, resulted in increased fishing pressure in other areas of the state.

After conducting extensive fish kill inventories, LDWF applied for and received $12,375,000 in Federal Dire Emergency Funds from Congress the following year. LDWF found it could now expand its plans and build a much larger, more comprehensive hatchery.

Federal monies covered the cost of construction, furnishings and equipment. These funds will also pay operating expenses for the next two to three years and contribute to the salaries of a full-time staff of eight.

Booker Fowler will produce all of the fry for Louisiana (except striped and hybrid striped bass) and most of the fingerlings. It will also raise its own forage, cutting that expense by two-thirds. The remaining three hatcheries, Beechwood, Monroe and LaCombe, will produce forage, some fingerlings and serve as rearing facilities.

Anglers will also be pleased to learn that Inland Fisheries intends to greatly expand the number of trophy and quality lakes around the state. Currently only three, Caney Lake, Lake Concordia and False River carry the distinction of trophy lakes. Seven waterbodies are designated as quality lakes. In time, each district of the state should have their own trophy lake, with bragging rights to boot.

They say that every cloud has a silver lining. Here's hoping that Hurricane Andrew was a dark cloud stitched with gold. ✦

BAD PRESS PROMPTS SEARCH FOR SAFER OYSTERS

STORY AND PHOTOGRAPHY BY JERALD HORST,
SEA GRANT MARINE AGENT

Louisiana has long had a love affair with the eastern oyster, *Crassostrea virginica*. Even Robert Maestri, the taciturn mayor of New Orleans in the late 1930s and early 1940s, would talk about oysters. Maestri was famous for his dislike of speeches and small talk. At a reception he hosted in New Orleans for the President of the United States, Franklin Delano Roosevelt, his only words to the president reportedly were "How ya like dem ersters?"

Louisianians are proud of their oysters and rightfully so. The Gulf Coast states produce between 60 and 70 percent of the nation's oysters, and Louisiana is by far the largest Gulf producer. In fact, Louisiana is usually the nation's largest oyster producer.

In recent years publicity over tainted or "bad" oysters has had people backing away from oyster bars en masse. The major reason, *V. vulnificus*, a naturally occurring brackish water and marine bacterium found on all U.S. coasts. Unfortunately, it is more active in the warmer waters of the Gulf Coast.

V. vulnificus is one of more than 60 species of vibrio bacteria. Eleven can cause illnesses in humans. Most common are *Vibrio cholera*

and *Vibrio parahaemolyticus*, both of which can cause intense diarrhea and other symptoms. Infections are usually caused by improper seafood handling, most often at home or by self-harvesters such as sport fishermen.

What sets *V. vulnificus* apart is that, in a very small portion of the human population, infection can result in death. While the death risk from eating raw Louisiana oysters is only one in 25 million raw oysters consumed, and even though 100 percent of the deaths have occurred in people with compromised immune-systems who shouldn't have been eating any raw protein product, the U.S. Food and Drug Administration (FDA) decided to take action.

First, they required prominent display of boldly worded warnings on tables and bars at establishments serving raw Gulf oysters. Not exactly something to whet one's appetite for raw oysters.

Then, adding injury to insult, a coalition which included the FDA and west coast oyster industries (Louisiana's oyster producing competitors) called for a complete ban on the harvest of Gulf oysters for raw consumption. This was proposed in spite of the fact that

What sets Vibrio vulnificus apart is that, in a very small portion of the human population, infection can result in death. While the death risk from eating raw Louisiana oysters is only one in 25 million raw oysters consumed, and even though 100 percent of the deaths have occurred in people with compromised immune-systems, the U.S. Food and Drug Administration (FDA) decided to take action.

Oysters coming into the AmeriPure plant (top) are graded for uniformity and trimmed of mussels and clutch shell. After washing, (middle) the trays are entered into a vat of water heated to a specific temperature for the pasteurization process. AmeriPure partner John Tesvich and Linda Andrews, plant manager and director of research, (bottom) hold a tray of processed oysters.

only about 10 deaths per year nationally, all of them among high-risk individuals, could be attributed to eating raw Gulf oysters.

Such a ban would devastate the state's oyster industry, which has an economic impact of over $100 million on the state, and break the hearts of hundreds of thousands of oyster loving Louisiana citizens and tourists as well as oyster connoisseurs throughout the nation.

Researchers in recent years have tried many methods to eliminate *V. vulnificus* from raw oysters. One process thought to be the answer was depuration, the holding of live oysters under controlled conditions in treated waters. The natural biological process of the oyster pumping this water through its system was expected to allow the oyster to "purge" itself of unwelcome bacteria.

While depuration was successful in reducing many bacteria, it was largely unsuccessful in removing *V. vulnificus*. Additionally, 10- to 15-percent of the oysters were lost during the three to four days of depuration.

Irradiation, while widely used on foods in Europe, is not approved in the United States for seafood. It requires an expensive facility and, even if successfully applied, may meet resistance from a public concerned about the safety of irradiated foods.

The use of FDA approved chemicals such as diacetyl, lactic acid and BHA showed promise in reducing bacterial levels. Unfortunately, some unpleasant flavors were a potential side effect.

Enter John Tesvich, a fourth-generation oyster farmer from Plaquemines Parish, Louisiana. In January 1995, Tesvich, along

with partners Patrick Fahey, a New Orleans-based businessman and former president of Delta Queen Steamboat Company, and John Schegan, president of Old New Orleans Seafood House, a southern California-based distributor of raw Gulf Coast oysters met with LSU Agricultural Center Sea Grant staffers Mike Moody and Paul Thibodaux and Ag Center Food Science researchers.

At that meeting, they discussed preliminary research done by Dr. David Chen at the FDA laboratory in Dauphin Island, AL. A proposal for research, funded by the three partners, was written to use a cool pasteurization process to reduce vibrio without affecting the taste and texture (sensory qualities) of oysters.

Between February and May, under the direction of Dr. Douglas Park, the Ag Center's principal investigator for the project, Ph.D student Brian Chen inoculated live oysters with vibrio and experimentally treated them over a 20 degree temperature range for various lengths of time.

The most effective temperature/time was adopted by Tesvich and his partners as the AmeriPure Process T/T. During the summer of 1995, the study was repeated with oysters with naturally occurring vibrio. The results were the same. *V. vulnificus* was reduced from levels "too numerous to count" to non-detectable levels.

Treatment involves dipping the oysters in hot water at a very specific temperature for a specific period of time. They are then plunged into 38 degrees Fahrenheit ice water to shock the bacteria.

The researchers now knew the process worked, but they had to determine if the process affected the taste and texture of the oysters. In the winter of 1995/96 an 11 member taste-test panel evaluated the AmeriPure Process oysters against raw untreated oysters. Evaluation was based on odor, color, texture and flavor.

The AmeriPure treated oysters were found to be slightly lighter in color, but the flavor, texture and smell were comparable to untreated oysters. The treated product was judged as highly acceptable. Some panelists actually preferred the treated oysters. An added benefit was that shelf life of the treated oysters was extended to 21 days, which is 7-10 days more than that for untreated oysters.

Tesvich, Fahey and Schegan constructed a pilot plant in Port Sulphur, LA for test marketing. At that time, Ralph and Kacoo's restaurants began serving AmeriPure oysters at their restaurants in Louisiana (except the French Quarter location), Mississippi and Alabama.

In July, the Louisiana Department of Health allowed the removal of warning labels associated with serving raw shellfish if the establishment served only treated oysters.

In October, a larger interim plant was established in Empire, LA to produce larger volumes of treated oysters to meet increasing demand. Construction of a permanent facility in Golden Meadow, LA is scheduled for this spring.

Besides Ralph and Kacoo's, AmeriPure oysters are available in several other restaurants and in selected grocery stores in the New Orleans area. As demand increases, AmeriPure plans to license other wholesalers to use the process. Consumers interested in learning who sells AmeriPure Process oysters may call **1-800-EAT M RAW (328-6729)**. Wholesalers interested in using the process should contact John Tesvich at 504/657-0474.

Consumers who are not "at risk" should feel comfortable in continuing to eat untreated raw oysters. "At risk" individuals are considered to be persons with any of the following conditions: Liver disease (including cirrhosis), alcoholism, cancer (especially during treatment), diabetes, kidney disease, chronic intestinal disease, steroid dependency (as used for conditions such as emphysema, etc.), achlorhydria (a condition of no or reduced stomach acid), AIDS, or abnormal iron metabolism.

As noted earlier, the small number of vibrio mortalities to date has been associated with "at risk" individuals. These same people should also avoid swimming or wading in brackish or saltwater if they have any skin damage such as cuts, wounds or burns. Nor should they clean or handle any raw seafood product that might puncture their skin.

Finally, thoroughly cooking seafood to an internal temperature of at least 140 degrees Fahrenheit allows even "at risk" individuals to consume oysters, as well as other seafood, without fear.

EDITOR'S NOTE: Oysters should be fried at a temperature of 375 degrees. ◆

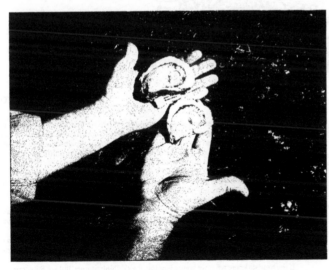

An AmeriPure processed oyster (left), compared to a raw oyster. Notice the uncooked or raw appearance of the processed oyster. In almost all characteristics, it approximates a raw oyster, except Vibrio is not present.

FREESTYLE FROGGING

BY HUMBERTO FONTOVA

F olklore has used swamps as a setting for everything that inspires dread in man's breast. Monsters, serpents, trolls, witches, escaped convicts, murderers—all of these have lurked in the shadowy depths of the swamp. Loathsome insects fluttered through its fetid air. Venomous reptiles slithered through its putrid muck. Its noxious waters spewed disease and poisonous vapors.

Just one generation ago, calling a swamp anything other than a reeking, disease-spawning, vermin-ridden pest hole fit only for filling or fumigation was to be labeled a crank or lunatic. Now half the brochures in any hotel lobby advertise swamp tours. Buses and pontoon boats line up to take smiling tourists into their moss-draped bowels.

Clutching cameras and camcorders and sporting florescent Bermudas and bateau-sized sneakers they pile onto buses headed for the boats that will ferry them through a panorama now celebrated almost nightly on the Discovery Channel or *National Geographic*.

Fred and I watched such a group loading up as we headed for a day of fishing and a night of frogging in the Manchac swamp. They reminded me of just one of the things we sportsmen often take for granted in south Louisiana—scenery.

If the tourists knew what we were planning, they'd think us nuts. But we think our kind of swamp tour beats the heck out of theirs. A swamp is best savored at night. That's when it truly becomes alive. Froggers know this. Especially those who frog from a pirogue. A motorboat or airboat would alert the swamp to our approach and presence. In a pirogue we're silent intruders, closing within feet of it's creatures. Some we will capture; most we will just observe.

We will glide into inky gloom with no engine racket to mar the nightly serenade. The chorus of chirps, croaks, grunts, peeps and wails from the swamp's natural dwellers comes to us with no background static. This is a swamp at it's most glorious, nature at it's rawest.

It's the only way to pursue frogs, if you ask us. A shallow draft pirogue also lets you access the weedier, shallower areas most favored by bull and pig frogs, our quarry. Two species here. The pig frog is smaller, slenderer, with more tolerance for brackish water and more of a preference for big water and deep swamps. You won't find many of them in roadside ditches, farm ponds or the overgrown puddles where you sometimes find the larger bullfrogs. Not that the southern bullfrog shuns deep swamps, but he's just as likely to turn up in a farm pond or suburban drainage canal.

Immersed in a swamp long after dark, a frogger can almost forget what he's after. Juicy, succulent froglegs become almost incidental. That brilliant beam stabbing through the blackness reveals other members of the nightly choir—the swamp owl peering down from the moss-draped tupelo branch; the red alligator eyes sliding over the bayou's surface before sinking in a silent swirl; the nutria, seemingly scratching but actually oiling his hide on the bank; the look of mild annoyance a raccoon rummaging in the shallows throws at the head-lamped intruder. "Hey buddy," he seems to say, "Who invited you?"

Then, as he nears the end of a slough the frogger can turn his gaze downward and probe the tea-clear water with light. Here he finds juvenile gars with splotched bodies finning slowly near the surface or floating almost motionless like logs. He spots a catfish probing the edge of a cypress stump for potential dinner. Yes, this is what a catfish looks like in it's native haunt. Amazing how long those whiskers stick out. Maybe one of those gators will still be motionless on the

bottom, waiting for the pest overhead to pass on by.

You can't see any of this from a car, or even from a pontoon boat in the daylight. Froggers in a pirogue see it on every trip.

After an afternoon of tussling with bluegills, we light a fire on the shore of Shell Bank bayou, not as much to heat our dinner as to ward off the bugs. Bugs are always at their worst during the first hour after dark. We've learned that by waiting till 9 p.m. and dousing ourselves liberally with repellent, they become a minor nuisance rather than a plague. But the bellowing of several bullfrogs was too much enticement and we shove off at 8:30 p.m., heading straight for the closest one.

The frogs are talkative tonight. Bullfrogs sound like someone groaning into an empty 50 gallon drum. Pig frogs have a shorter, sharper grunt, almost like a pig. Hence the name. We can hear a chorus of both as we paddled. This is a mixed blessing.

Only frogs that are partly in water seem to bellow. With so many bellowing we feared the worst—a high tide that scatters them. We swept our headlamps across the slough and several pairs of eyes glowed back. But these shone pink and most were well out into the water. As we came alongside the closest one the gator ducked but stayed motionless on the bottom a scant two feet below. The gator was perfectly visible through water that entered muddy from Pass Manchac but was filtered by miles of swamp vegetation to the color of watery root beer. We halted and studied the gator's every detail through the clear water. I bumped the pirogue with the

Ideally, when frogging on sloughs, canals and bayous you want a low tide which exposes an area of mud between the grassy bank and the water. The frogs come to the edge of the water, which means exposing themselves on the mud bank.

paddle and he flattened his legs against his body. Then with slow undulating sweeps of his tail swam off.

Back to the business at hand. "Forget it," Fred snorted as we probed the bank with our lights. "That frog is WAY back up in there. We'll never find him. Let's keep going."

Ditto the next two. The tide was high, courtesy of three days of strong southeast winds. This floods the swamp and scatters the frogs. Great for them but not so great for us. Ideally, when frogging on sloughs, canals and bayous you want a low tide which exposes an area of mud between the grassy bank and the water. The frogs come to the edge of the water, which means exposing themselves on the mud bank. Finding and catching them becomes a cakewalk. But no such luck tonight. We'd have to work for our culinary reward.

Some grunts seemed to come from just a few feet ahead, but our beams revealed nothing through the wall of smartweed. Exasperated I stood in the pirogue using my paddle for leverage and looked down into the grass. Sure enough, a pair of bright green

Adult bullfrogs in south Louisiana feed primarily on crawfish. A place that looks good for crawfishing is probably also good for frogging.
LDWF file photo

eyes shone back. He was a monster. "He's right in front of you." I pointed to Fred who was in front. "Here's the gig." "I don't need that." He quipped. "Watch." Then he kneeled in the very front while I steadied the pirogue with the paddle. All I could see was Fred's wet rear and his outstretched arm. But certainly his face was a mask of grim resolution, like a cat stalking a squirrel ... He pounced and - YES - up with a colossal bullfrog, it's legs pumping

in futility and its skin glistening under our lights. "This!" Fred beams, "Is how the pros do it!"

We ended up two hours later with only 10, but they were all beauties. We had to find them in the flooded smartweed and alligator grass, often by crawling out of the pirogue into the flooded swamp. An exciting night. Beats the heck out of the movies.

Bull and pig frogs seem to love areas that are just a little too deep or soft to walk through and too clogged to float through. The more clogged with hyacinths, alligator grass, smartweed, etc. the more frogs it holds. A pirogue gives best access to such places. On more open waterways like bayous or canals, those with the bushiest banks will hold the most frogs. Streams that run through swamps or woods with a closed canopy of trees aren't the best for frogging. They might be easy to paddle through and picturesque, but the lack of underbrush near the stream banks make for low frog populations. We've noticed this time and again.

Adult bullfrogs in south Louisiana feed primarily on crawfish. The young ones on insects. A place that looks good for crawfishing is probably also good for frogging. The lower Atchafalaya basin is a perfect example. The famous basin crawfish nourishes probably the biggest population of bullfrogs in Louisiana. The last couple of years however, have seen relatively few frogs in this area. Jeff Boundy, a biologist specializing in reptiles and amphibians for the Department of Wildlife and Fisheries, attributes this to harsh winters. "Frog populations are cyclical," he says. "Much like rabbits. We've had two bad winters in a row. This past one was fairly mild. So depending on what we find this season we'll see if the freezes were the reason for their decline."

The cost of outfitting for frogging isn't likely to spark marital discord. A gig either of the stabbing or grabbing kind at the end of the longest pole you can find, a headlamp attached to a 6 or 12 volt battery. hip boots and a wire fish basket or sack. That's about it. And as we saw earlier, the gig is actually optional. Just be sure its a frog before you grab.

EDITOR'S NOTE: Frogging is not allowed during the months of April and May in Louisiana. Frogging regulations are included in the 1997 Louisiana Fishing Regulations pamphlet.

Mixing It Up
in Coastal Marshes

STORY & PHOTOGRAPHY
BY JOHN FELSHER

Mike Herrmann dropped a spinnerbait into a weedy patch along a broken Delacroix marsh shoreline. Retrieving steadily, the lure buzzed just beneath the surface.

From beneath the grass, a black object spotted the offer and homed in like a torpedo. WHAM! Water erupted in frothy fury as another big-mouthed beast devoured the bait. This fish happened to be a 2-pound largemouth bass. On another cast, it might have been an 8-pound redfish.

In the stern, I worked a gold rapala along a weedy bank. Flashing silver, a trout slashed into the lure, nearly ripping the rod from my hand. Breaking water, this fish showed its spots — literally.

Within only a few feet and nearly simultaneously, we both boated fish, a bass and a speckled trout. Wait a minute. Bass live in freshwater and speckled trout live in brine. What's going on, some freak life-altering atmospheric condition? Hardly!

"On one cast, you can catch a redfish. On the next cast, you can catch a bass. On the third cast, you can catch a speckled trout. That happens to me all the time," said Herrmann, who runs Louisiana Fish and Fowl Guide Service in Chalmette.

Ostensibly fishing for bass, we didn't mind lightning speckled trout strikes or the brutal power of redfish. On this particular morning, we caught four species - largemouth bass, speckled trout, redfish, and hybrid bass. On other occasions, we may easily have boated striped bass, flounder, croaker, white trout, black drum, sheepshead, white and black crappie, bluegills, redear sunfish, gafftopsail catfish, channel catfish, blue catfish and perhaps a dozen other species.

Far from unique to Delacroix, catching both freshwater and marine species in the same place commonly occurs across Louisiana's coastal marshes. From the Pearl River. estuary to the Sabine, Bayou State anglers can enjoy outstanding fishing for both fresh and saltwater species at the same time and in the same place.

"On the northern part of Pointe-Au-Chien Wildlife Management Area near Houma, I've seen people catch bass and bream while I'm fishing for speckled trout and redfish," said Andre LaFosse, a fisheries specialist for the Louisiana Department of Wildlife and Fisheries. "Sometimes people in the same boat catch different species, depending on the bait they are using. One day, I fished with cacohoe minnows and caught a three-pound bass, a three-pound speck, a choupique, a

blue catfish and a redfish all off one stick near shore."

God blessed Louisiana with many rivers and bayous that empty into the Gulf of Mexico, directly or indirectly. In marshes, brown freshwater from rivers and bayous meets the green Gulf brine. The result creates a lush brackish smorgasbord containing elements of both fresh and saltwater.

"There is a line across the state where freshwater ends and saltwater begins. It's not a straight line; it fluctuates with freshwater flow," LaFosse said. "In that brackish range, you can catch everything from bream, sac-a-lait, bass and catfish, to speckled trout, redfish and sheepshead in the same spot. The water is livable for both types of fish, salt and fresh."

"Depending upon salinity or freshwater flows out of rivers, you'll get both freshwater and estuarine species. It's quite common to catch a bass on one cast and a speckled trout on the next," said Bobby Reed, LDWF district fisheries biologist in Lake Charles.

Obviously, the greatest mixing source comes from the Mississippi River itself. Draining two-thirds of the nation, an enormous freshwater gush sweetens the gulf for miles. At Venice, near the delta, anglers find a multi-species paradise unlike any other in this country.

"People catch bass, stripers, redfish, speckled trout, all species. In the Mississippi River, near the intersection of Venice Marina and the Mississippi river at the Jump, there are many rocks. You don't know what you are going to catch. In the river itself on a Rat-L-Trap, I've caught bass, specks, reds, flounder and stripers," LaFosse said.

Throughout Louisiana, various species co-exist in these transitional areas. Wherever large volumes of freshwater dump into marshes, salt and freshwater species feed on each other.

"In brackish water, there is enough salinity for speckled trout and redfish to feed", Reed said. "They enter fresh water quite readily to feed. Bass can tolerate short term salinity of two to three parts per thousand. At certain tides, the water is right where all these fish can mix together. There is a transition or gradient zone where both live. It's a coastal phenomenon."

Both fish types feed on abundant forage in coastal marshes. They can feast on freshwater forage like grass shrimp, crawfish, minnows and young sunfish or munch marine morsels like crabs, shrimp, cacohoe minnows, croakers or a thousand other creatures. Frequently, bass attack a school of baitfish from one side while redfish and speckled trout hit them from another side. Beneath the school, flounder wait for cripples to fall to the bottom. Large catfish scoop up the leavings.

"They could all feed on the school at the same time," Reed said.

"Bass and reds feed on mullets, shrimp, cacohoe minnows, grass shrimp, crabs. There is a lot of food in the marsh. You've got

Louisiana Conservationist Magazine

A great addition for the outdoors person who has everything. Published six times a year with 36 pages of full color photographs and informative articles on fishing, hunting and outdoor activities, along with news updates on wildlife and fisheries rules and regulations.

Subscriptions: 1 year - $10, 2 years - $18, 4 years - $30.

The Official Louisiana Seafood & Wild Game Cookbook.

A collection of more than 450 delectable, time-tested Louisiana dishes. Recipes for all types of wild game as well as side dishes and desserts. Color photographs.
$13.95 *SALE $10.50*

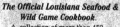

Managing White-tails in Louisiana

In-depth information on deer management in Louisiana. A guide for landowners, hunting clubs and individuals. Soft cover. Spiral bound. 95 pages.
$5.00

Louisiana Conservationist Caps and Patch

One size fits all. Available in white only with a *Louisiana Conservationist* patch. $5.00 *SALE $3.50*
Embroidered patch only. $1.00 *SALE $ .50*

NEW! Louisiana Department of Wildlife & Fisheries Belt Buckle

Heavy solid brass emblazoned with the department's logo. Measures 2 1/8" x 3 1/4".
$12.50

Antiqued Pewter Pins

Hand crafted pewter pins in two sizes. Full size pins average 2" x 1" and mini pins average 3/4" x 1/2". Each full size pin has two clasps on the back to keep it from moving.
Specify number and name when ordering

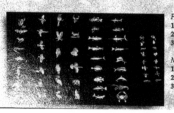

Full size pins
1 - $6.00 each
2 - $5.00 each
3 plus $5.50 each

Mini pins
1 - $3.00 each
2 - $2.50 each
3 plus $2.25 each

Full size pins available:

100 Channel catfish	222 Flounder	361 Snowy owl
102 Crappie	227 Redfish	372 Blue jay
111 Sunfish	269 Sea horse	402 White-tail deer
140 Bass	301 Pheasant	405 Black bear
141 Largemouth bass	304 Woodcock	414 Otter
152 Paddlefish	308 Turkey	416 Armadillo
201 Sailfish	321 Mallard	421 White-tail (8 pt.)
203 Dolphin fish	326 Turkey	475 Dolphin (porpoise)
204 Shark	329 Bobwhite	499 Bat
207 Striped bass	331 Bald eagle	527 Crawfish
209 Tarpon	342 Pelican	531 Crab
211 Speck (weakfish)	345 Great blue heron	571 Luna moth
214 Redfish	350 Hummingbird	591 Tree frog
217 Swordfish	351 Dove	600 Alligator
219 King mackerel	360 Horned owl	607 Sea turtle

Mini pins available:

M140 Bass	M321 Mallard	M420 Buck
M304 Woodcock	M329 Quail	M530 Lobster

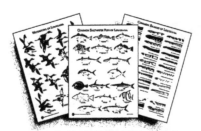

Louisiana Wildlife & Fisheries Posters
Seven different posters available: Waterfowl, freshwater fish,
offshore fish, saltwater fish, snakes, amphibians, turtles.
Any combination: 1-2 posters $4.00 each; 3-6 posters $3.50 each;
7 or more $3.00 each.   Poster size: 17" x 22"

Louisiana Butterflies
Full color photographs of 41 species with
scientific names, common names and host
plants. Poster size: 25" x 36" *Limited supply*
(Frame not included)
$5.00

Atchafalaya Basin Map
Detailed drawing of the basin
including the Atchafalaya Delta
Wildlife Management Area.
*Specify folded or rolled when
ordering.*   **$1.50**

Marine Recreational
Fishing Maps
Five in a series of six maps are
available. Each full color map
indicates offshore/inshore rig
locations, launches, marinas, fishing tips and species
identification. Each map covers a specialized area:
#1 Venice to Fourchon; #2 Fourchon to Point Au Fer;
#3 Lake Pontchartrain to Chandeleur Sound;
#4 Sabine Pass to White Lake;
#5 White Lake to Atchafalaya Bay.
Specify map number and choice of rolled or folded.
$11.00 each

NEW! Bats of the
Eastern United States
Full color photographs
of species with
scientific and common
names. Bat facts are
listed on the backside of
the poster. Instructions
for building a bat house
are included. Poster size:
24" x 36"   **$2.50**

Louisiana Conservationist Bumper sticker $1.00 SALE $ .50

Form 1

May we substitute color?   **Subtotal** _____

Yes ____ No____

1st choice _____   Shipping & Handling *(see chart)* _____

2nd choice _____   Tax (4% for Louisiana residents) _____

       Additional 4% tax for EBR Parish residents _____

       Total Amount Due _____

Ship To:

Name _____

Address _____

City _____ State _____

Zip _____ Daytime Phone (___) _____

PAYMENT METHOD
❑Check/Money Order   ❑MasterCard   ❑VISA

Credit Card Information

Account No. _____

Expiration Date _____

Signature _____

Shipping & Handling Charges *These charges DO NOT apply to the commemorative knife.*	
Merchandise Total	Charge
Up to $15.00	$3.50
$15.01-$30.00	$5.25
$30.01-$45.00	$6.50
$45.01-$65.00	$8.00
$65.01-$95.00	$9.50
$95.01 and up	$11.00

Send orders (checks payable to);
Louisiana Conservationist
Marketing Unit
P.O. Box 98000
Baton Rouge, LA 70898

Allow 4 to 6 weeks for delivery. Prices subject to change without notice. Defective or damaged merchandise only will be refunded or exchanged for same product.

Form 2

	Quantity	Price	Subtotal
Commemorative Knife		$150.00	
		Total	
Shipping & Handling $5.00 *per knife*			
4% tax for Louisiana residents			
Additional 4% tax for EBR Parish residents			
TOTAL AMOUNT DUE			

Ship To:

Name _____

Address _____

City _____ State _____

Zip _____ Daytime Phone (___) _____

PAYMENT METHOD
❑Check/Money Order   ❑MasterCard   ❑VISA

Credit Card Information

Account No. _____

Expiration Date _____

Signature _____

Send order (checks payable to):
Louisiana Conservationist
Commemorative Knife
P.O. Box 98000

Serial numbers are assigned as orders are received. "Reserved" serial numbers or special marking/engraving will not be available. Please remember that these knives are painstakingly hand crafted and no two are identical. Your knife will be shipped via UPS/insured as soon as it is delivered to us by the knife maker. Your patience is appreciated.

Form 3

Send magazine to:

Name _____

Address _____

City _____ State _____ Zip _____

Phone _____

Gift Giver:

Name _____

Address _____

City _____ State _____ Zip _____

Phone _____

PAYMENT METHOD

❑New   ❑ $10 one year   ❑ Check/money

❑Gift   ❑ $18 two years   ❑ MasterCard

❑Renewal   ❑ $30 four years   ❑ VISA

If MasterCard or VISA, give information below:

Acct# _____

Signature _____ Exp. Date _____

Send your order (checks payable to):
Louisiana Conservationist
P.O. Box 98000
Baton Rouge, LA 70898-9000

all the freshwater stuff and saltwater stuff," Herrmann said.

Lure fishermen generally use similar tactics for speckled trout, redfish and bass. All three species readily hit similar lures.

"The most popular bait in Delacroix is a 3/4-ounce Johnson silver minnow. We tie it to a barrel swivel with a six-inch leader to keep it from twisting. That works very well in areas where grass is pretty heavy. You'll catch bass, redfish and trout on that," Herrmann said. "I use the same bass tactics for reds. I use spinnerbaits, buzzbaits, Rat-L-Traps, plastic worms. Purple is my favorite color year-round."

"Plastic worms and slow running grubs bounced off the bottom are good for flounder, especially if you put a little shrimp on the end," LaFosse said.

In addition, anglers using either live shrimp or minnows catch crappie, sheepshead, flounder, catfish, white bass, yellow bass and maybe stripers. Using cut bait or fresh shrimp, anglers catch those species plus gafftopsail catfish, black drum, bream and many other species.

Nothing dominates the marsh ecosystem like tides. They dictate nearly everything that happens in the reedy shallows and may determine fish types in an area. A high tide brings marine species in closer and pushes bass and other freshwater species deeper into the marsh. When tides fall, enormous quantities of baitfish, shrimp, crabs and other forage literally flow into predator's mouths. At lagoon openings, various species gather for lunch to drop in on them.

"Outgoing tides in certain areas are better," thinks LaFosse. "There are bays and small ponds all over the marsh. When tides fall, baitfish in those ponds get pulled out of those drains into the main water bodies. At these drains, fishing is better because fish stack up there waiting to feed. If I had to pick either one, I would pick a falling tide for freshwater fish. Shrimp and small crabs don't have much control over a strong tide. They get pulled easily and fish are right there ready to eat."

Reed says it doesn't matter if the tide moves out or in, as long as it is moving.

"Both fresh and saltwater fish tend to feed better when the tide is moving, either falling or rising. Avoid a slack tide. That's probably because the food source is moving with rising or falling tides. Fish take advantage of forage moving around and they feed better," the biologist said.

Although bass thrive upon abundant food in rich tidal marshes, they often don't reach great size like their reservoir cousins. Biologists think that environmental harshness may affect them.

"The marsh is a shallow, hostile environment subject to rapid changes. It can be extremely hot in summer and extremely cold in winter. It is high in organic matter and that tends to lead to low oxygen problems. There is more competition for food and space in the marsh. Bass aren't the top carnivores in the marsh. They are mixed in with everything else, like choupique, blue cat and gars. Their life span is just not as long because the environment is so hostile, but while they are alive, they are quite lively and robust fish," Reed said.

Across Louisiana, it is impossible to tell where freshwater ends and brine begins, especially when diverse species intermingle. While the state drew a line and declared a legal demarcation, true demarcation fluctuates daily and is always accompanied by a broad, brackish mixing zone.

To fish for saltwater species south of the line, anglers must purchase a saltwater license along with a basic fishing license. The law states: "All recreational anglers fishing south of the saltwater line for saltwater species must have in their possession a Louisiana saltwater anglers license in addition to a basic Louisiana fishing license except those persons exempted from purchasing a regular Louisiana fishing license."

"I would recommend fishermen go ahead and purchase the $5.50 saltwater license so they don't have to worry about crossing the zone," Reed said.

Once they purchase that license, anglers can enjoy the best of both worlds by catching both fresh and saltwater species on the same trip. With so many species available, if your preferred species isn't biting, something else probably is. ⬩

Mike Herrmann of Chalmette hefts a hybrid white bass caught in Louisiana marshes near Delacroix.

Bag Your Own Bait

Use a Cast Net

STORY & PHOTOGRAPHY BY DON DUBUC

I t's called the great debate. Or is it "de-bait"? Live bait versus artificial bait discussions will probably continue as long as there are fish and fishermen. Even the most dedicated live bait enthusiast will admit there are times under certain conditions when fish, for whatever strange reasons, prefer plastic to the real thing. And not many will argue that artificial bait isn't cleaner, quicker and in many cases, less expensive. Then there are those times when redfish or speckled trout will have nothing to do with soft or hard plastics and only want Mother Nature's originals. It can be a pretty frustrating feeling when anglers in the next boat are hauling in fish with every cast while your artificials go untouched regardless how enticing you make them seem.

There are only two ways to secure live bait — buy it or catch it. Live shrimp this summer hit an all-time high of 20 cents apiece at many places along the Louisiana coast. Minnows were not far behind at 15 cents each. Commercial live bait dealers are faced with escalating expenses as well as physical effort to catch bait and keep it lively. No doubt the spiraling, upward cost of live bait will continue as the costs of fuel, nets and labor also rise.

The alternative is to catch your own and many sport fishermen are doing just that. It only involves the modest price of a cast net and a few minutes just prior to your trip. Minnow traps work well for certain baitfish but they require the fish to come to the trap. Cast netting allows the angler to go after the bait wherever they may be.

A cast net is a fine mesh net weighted on the bottom with leads spaced several inches apart. It is a circular net that fans out when thrown over a school of baitfish. The lead weights cause it to sink rapidly over the bait. As it is retrieved with a hand line tied to the top, the weights pull the bottom opening shut, entrapping the fish within.

Shrimp and cacaho minnows are the most popular baits for saltwater fishing but there are others equally as good if not better under particular conditions.

Cacaho minnows, while usually available year round at bait shops, marinas and boat launches, are probably the hardest species to catch with a cast net. Sportsmen will probably have more success with a couple of traps placed in the marsh.

Shrimp can easily be caught with a cast net but must be located or attracted to a pier, dock or bank. Baiting for shrimp can easily be done with canned dog food or cracked clams. Lighted docks are excellent spots to catch shrimp and other baits at night.

Menhaden, also known as pogies, under four inches long are very good bait for speckled trout, redfish and black drum. The Menhaden is a small, flat, silvery fish with a black dot on the side just behind the head. It has a relatively small mouth for its size and closely resembles domestic sardines. It is a very fragile fish and should be gently handled when removed from the net. A good aerator is necessary to keep them lively.

Pogies will congregate in calm canals during the warmer months. Cast nets should be thrown from the bow of the boat either drifting or powered by a trolling motor. The trolling method is preferred since the boat can be controlled to follow surface activity, a tell-tale sign that pogies are in the area.

For redfish, the striped mullet is hard to beat. Mullet are bullet-shaped fish with black and silver stripes. The smaller ones, called finger mullet, are good for rat reds while the larger mullets (8-14 inches) are excellent for bull reds when fished whole or cut in chunks.

During the summer months, striped mullets can be found in or near passes close to the coastal beaches. Their habit of floating just under the surface makes them easy to spot.

A particularly good nighttime bait for speckled trout is the glass minnow, also known as the silverside minnow. They are also excellent bait for spanish mackerel. These small, long, translucent baitfish are most easily identified by a silver stripe running from head to tail. They can often be caught with cast nets at night around lighted piers. The cast net must be retrieved very quickly because glass minnows are very thin and pass through mesh easily. A long-handled, small mesh dip net sometimes will work better than a cast net.

Another especially good bait for speckled trout in late summer and early fall are small croakers. Because they are open water fish they can be difficult to locate and catch with a cast net. However, they can frequently be netted in very small marsh cuts connecting ponds or lagoons during periods of falling tide. Besides cast nets, recreational trawls used in open canals or small lakes can be an effective method of catching baby croakers.

Throwing a cast net is a skill that requires repeated practice. The key is to get the net to open fully to maximize its efficiency.

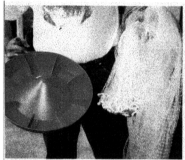

An alternative to hand-throwing a cast net is the use of a net pan. The idea is to align the net in such a way as to easily toss it into a near perfect circle.

Modern cast nets are fashioned from nylon, usually monofilament strands. Gone are the days of the old cotton nets. Except for a few hobbyists, cast net knitting by hand has gone the way of the dinosaurs. Cost, durability and light weight make today's nylon nets much more practical than the cotton nets of days gone by.

Monofilament and multi-strand nylon nets come in a variety of sizes. Popular mesh sizes are 3/8", 3/4" and for offshore use, 1/2", according to Gus Maggiore Jr., owner of Gus' Tackle & Nets in Slidell.

"We handle four, five, six, seven, eight and 12-foot radius nets. The eight foot size is the most popular with recreational bait fishermen and shrimpers," Maggiore said. "The smaller the net, the easier it is to throw. Of course the wider the net, the greater the chance to encircle bait."

Throwing a cast net is a skill that requires repeated practice. The key is to get the net to open fully to maximize its efficiency. A line tied to the wrist prevents the net from being lost and allows the person to retrieve it.

To properly throw a cast net, the top of the net is held in one hand along with several sections divided by the lead weights. In the other hand the other end of the net with the remaining sections is held. Some throwers like to hold the middle section of the net between their teeth giving them a "third hand" to help spread the net better. Let me caution you there is danger involved with this practice. Clear, almost invisible, jellyfish are often snagged in cast nets when thrown in saltier waters. The sting of a jellyfish on the lips and gums can be quite painful.

There are a number of "recommended" methods of throwing a cast net. One is illustrated here as an example:

An alternative to hand-throwing a cast net is the use of a net pan. This device is a round, plastic pan with dividers inside and a molded, plastic handle on the outside. The idea is to align the net in such a way as to easily toss it into a near perfect circle.

To load a net pan with a soft nylon net, grasp the net approximately three or four feet above the weighted lead line and drop the leads into the pan, being sure they are equally distributed into the divided sections. In a clockwise motion, curl the net in a circle on top of the pan, having the hand line exit the pan on your side of the handle. Attach the other end of the hand line to your left wrist with a rubber band for safety reasons. Pick up the pan with both hands, trapping the net end of the line with your right wrist. Left handers should reverse the procedure.

To cast the net from the pan, hold the "loaded" pan about waist level, rotate your body to the left (like a discus thrower) and encircle the pan with your right arm. Using a smooth upward, frisbee-type throw, cast the net forward at a 45 degree angle while releasing the hand opposite the handle. The net will leave the pan and open into a circle. Left handers can adapt these directions for their use. It sounds much more complicated than it is. Throwing a cast net takes only a little more skill than a frisbee. Again, practice is essential.

Whether using a net pan or hand throwing, the object is to have the net hit the water fully opened. Distance is not as important as a good wide opening. It really takes little physical effort to throw the net and a common mistake made by beginners is to throw too hard. A heavy wind in your face will make throwing extremely difficult. Always throw with the wind at your back.

Regulations governing the use of cast nets in Louisiana are few and fairly simple. Recreational cast netters must have a basic recreational fishing license and a saltwater fishing license in their possession and may use nets 8 1/2 feet or less in radius (17 feet maximum diameter) for the purpose of taking minnows, shrimp and other baits. If you are after freshwater baits above the state's official saltwater demarcation line, only the basic recreational fishing license is required. Properly licensed commercial fishermen are allowed to use larger cast nets, but must purchase a special cast net/dip net license.

Treatise on a Monarch

STORY & PHOTOGRAPHY BY PETE COOPER JR.

I t is time for Louisiana anglers to seek the company of kings in the waters around the Mississippi River Delta.

I'm sure most of you are familiar with the TV commercial: A group of guys have ended a day of some outdoor activity. One of them reaches into a cooler for a can of liquid refreshment, pops the top, takes a swallow, then gazes across the landscape and declares, "You know, it just doesn't get any better than this."

Wrong! Here in Louisiana we have several — nay, numerous outdoor opportunities far above those I have seen on TV. One in particular rates among the best in the entire world! It is a great and oft times fierce battle with high royalty: a king clad in silver mail. But unlike in days of yore, the object now is not to kill him but to count coup — to touch him, then allow him to return to his watery halls. It is fishing for tarpon.

I tend to wax a bit emotional when I write of tarpon — something I enjoy almost as much as fishing for them. I was smitten by tarpon at a very early age, in the course of three brief but treasured encounters with them near Rockport on the Texas coast. But I did not actually touch my first until I was almost forty. I must confess to killing it — 151 pounds. Since then I have touched 12 others, one on fly tackle and four of which were estimated to be in excess of 150 pounds — the largest of which "taped" 190. All were set free hopefully none the worse for wear.

I will fish for them at literally any and every opportunity. Often I simply go along to watch others fish for them — to watch the spectacle of the silver king's awesome struggle for his freedom. For me, and many like me, there

is nothing comparable in the world of fishing.

Thirteen fish do not make one an authority on them, but they have sure strengthened the feelings fermenting in my breast for so long, some of which have proven to be quite contagious.

Barbara keeps in close touch with her two brothers. The tales she has related to brother John over the years of my "most-recent fish" finally got to his head. Last September he came down from Missouri for a visit and brought along an obsession to catch a tarpon. In one and one-half days with Capt. Brent Ballay in the West Delta

area, he caught three — the largest around 150 pounds. For the remainder of his stay, his feet never touched the ground. His face was set in a permanent smile and his head slowly shook from side to side in amazement. John now has a glassed-in table in his living room full of pictures and mementos of those fish. I am told all his friends have heard his tales of those two days so often that they know them word for word. Poor John. It's tough enough for one as close to them as I am to be smitten by them, but to be from Missouri? I have little doubt we shall have a visitor again next September.

as early as April? It's real iffy, but in 1994 I had the rare privilege of catching the first fish of the year. Dave Ballay followed shortly with the second. That was a day I will never forget. It was the vanguard of what would become the masses of summer and they were hungry! We jumped nine. Three of them, including the one of mine which we brought to boatside, were on a fly!

You may also be familiar with some of the names of the Tarpon Legion, a few of whom might now be considered legends: Dave and Debbie Ballay, Pappa Joe Schouest and his son Lance (the near-famous "Coon" who invented the "Coon Pop", a lure so effective it is now used almost exclusively and has been mimicked by numerous others).

Undoubtedly some of you fish for tarpon; a few of you may even be among the smitten. My intent with these lines is not to inform you of the particulars, as it is a rather expensive sport to gear up for and requires a lot of time to learn, but to inspire you to go, to meet the silver king and to marvel at him. And your best chance for that is on a charter boat.

· Since much of the best action throughout the season occurs within the middle reaches of West Delta and at Southwest Pass, boats based in both Grand Isle and Venice can get there in a hurry. The melee John, Brent and I experienced last September took place barely seven miles from the mouth of Tiger Pass. From either port, a long run is not required to reach this area.

Prime time is also the period of our most settled weather. Assuredly there will be squalls, but tropical activity gives plenty of forewarning and usually any complaints about "conditions" are directed more toward the heat than lumpy seas. Sunscreen and plenty of Gatorade and the like is much more important now than Dramamine, though a couple of these stuck in a shirt pocket, just in case, are a good idea.

All the tackle, lures and such are provided by the boats, as are full

They do that to you. Imagine a hot, hazy, summer sunrise literally surrounded by hundreds of crashing, gulping, broaching, free-jumping tarpon, three rods down and two fish in the air at once just off the stern — then again — and again — performing like synchronized acrobats. Then with that pair subdued, revived, and released (don't recall what happened with the third rod, but the line probably tangled and broke), within 10 minutes another pair was churning the surface of West Delta into a froth. Super stuff. A true "melee" — and it does not get any better than that!

It is likely many of you have read of Louisiana's tarpon in these and other pages. They are certainly no secret. The names of the particular places they are most often found have become synonymous with them, conjuring memories and fantasies within the devoted of melees and glorious aerial displays: West Delta, Southwest Pass, the South Pass Mud Lumps and Northeast Pass. The most opportune time for world class fish, August and September, is also well known. Aspiring novices and experienced tarpon anglers from throughout the country come to the Delta during that period to fish for them.

But did you know they can arrive

60 YEAR OLD FEDERAL PROGRAM MEANS BIG $ FOR LOUISIANA

BY **CLIFTON COLES**

Photo by Gary Kramer

Most of the nation's hunters have heard of the Pittman-Robertson Program. If they haven't they should have, since it is hunters who are the driving force behind the program, which funds many aspects of the outdoor activities they enjoy.

1997 marks the sixtieth year of Pittman-Robertson — 60 years of restoration, reclamation, conservation and education for the nation's outdoorsmen and outdoorswomen. Every time you plunk down your greenbacks to buy certain types of hunting equipment and ammunition, a portion of your money is used for enhancement of the woods and wildlife habitat we all love, need and appreciate. It is the perfect example of a user-fee program with hunters being both the source and the beneficiary of funds used to enhance outdoor activities across the nation.

Most importantly to Louisiana hunters is the nationwide increase in white-tailed deer and wood duck populations. The national deer population is 36 times greater than it was in 1937. Wood ducks were feared extinct and hunting was banned in 1920. Today, they are the most common breeding waterfowl in the East and are able to sustain a healthy annual harvest.

The Pittman-Robertson Act (officially the Federal Aid in Wildlife Restoration Act) began as a federal law signed in 1937 by President Franklin D. Roosevelt. The law accomplished three things: (1) apportioned federal firearms and ammunition taxes to the states on a matching basis based on the number of hunting licenses sold and state size, up to $3 P-R funding for every $1 state "matching" funding; (2) prohibited use of P-R revenue for any purpose other than wildlife conservation; and (3) prohibited states from using their hunting license fees for any purpose other than supporting the state fish and game agency.

The year after ratification, three types of state projects eligible for funding were spelled out: (1) purchase of land for wildlife rehabilitation; (2) development of land to make it more suitable for wild mammals and birds; and (3) research.

Hunters nationwide pay an excise tax collected at the manufacturers' level on sporting rifles, shotguns, handguns, ammunition and archery hunting equipment. The money generated is funneled into programs that educate the public in safety afield and enhance habitat and environment, providing for more recreational opportunities. This fuels even higher consumption of equipment and goods.

This cyclical process is repeated across the nation. Each state's allotted share is based on state size and the number of annual licenses sold. All 50 states and five territories (Puerto Rico, Guam, the Virgin Islands, American Samoa and the Northern Mariana Islands) receive a share.

The Federal Aid in Sport Fish Restoration Act (Dingell-Johnson/Wallop-Breaux) was enacted in 1950 on the same lines. The Teaming with Wildlife initiative, which is in the beginning stages of development, will work in the same way with emphasis on non-game species.

The Federal Aid in Wildlife Restoration Program boasts many nationwide successes, including pronghorn antelope (whose population is now 83 times greater) and Rocky Mountain elk (whose population has grown 19.5 times). Other achievements include flourishing pheasant, caribou, bobcat, mountain lion, black bear and bighorn sheep populations, as well as birds of prey and songbirds that have benefitted along the way.

Most importantly to Louisiana hunters is the nationwide increase in white-tailed deer, wild turkey and wood duck populations. The national deer population is 36 times greater than it was in 1937, up from 500,000 to 18 million animals. The turkey population has grown a whopping 45 times since the program's inception, from 100,000 to 4.5 million. Wood ducks were feared extinct and hunting was banned in 1920. Today, they are the most common breeding waterfowl in the East and are able to sustain a healthy annual harvest.

Today's Louisiana deer herd exceeds what only a few decades ago was the total for the entire United States. Louisiana's turkey population has leapt from a paltry 1,500 in the 1940s to well over 25,000 today.

The number of hunters has tripled since the inception of the program. In 60 years, $4 billion have been distributed to the states to help restore dwindling species populations, acquire millions of acres of habitat and educate hundreds of thousands of hunters.

The sale of more than 250,000 hunting licenses purchased in Louisiana in 1995-96 is used to help determine the state's monetary share in the Pittman-Robertson program. Figures have not been finalized at the time this article went to press, but Louisiana's preliminary apportionment, according to the U.S. Department of the Interior, totals $2.1 million, $1.6 million of which will go to wildlife restoration and the rest to Hunter Education.

To date, Louisiana has received $56.4 million in apportionment funds. The Department of Wildlife and Fisheries is the state agency responsible for receiving and utilizing P-R funds.

Approximately one-fourth of LDWF's latest P-R allotment ($523,000) is devoted to Hunter Education, which reaches more than 20,000 students annually. The Department's Hunter Education program operates year-round, instructing youngsters in the basics of safety, outdoor ethics, wildlife management and habitat preferences of game species, selecting a firearm, and handling and maintaining firearms. These are skills and knowledge that will stay with the hunter for a lifetime, making the state's woods and fields safer for present and future generations.

Certification is required of everyone born on or after Sept. 1, 1969 in order to legally purchase a Louisiana hunting license, but Chester Carpenter, LDWF Hunter Education Coordinator, recommends that everyone take the course regardless of age.

"It's probably not a bad idea to take a refresher," he said. "It may make you a better hunter and will instill in your children and other young people the importance of hunting safety."

Hunter Education programs are conducted free of charge. When you go, you receive books and brochures along with first-class instruction and hands-on firearm training. It costs nothing at the time, but you and your fellow hunters have or will contribute to the continuance of this vital program through your excise tax dollars.

Sportsmen's dollars also provided the $200,000 needed to build a wildlife education center at the state's first urban refuge. Baton Rouge's 237-acre Waddill Wildlife Refuge has been designated for the new center. It will be a classroom facility for hunter education and other classes and basic and advanced training programs and activities for the public and Department employees. LDWF Education Manager Bob Penley anticipates that the classroom will serve more than 1,500 people from East Baton Rouge and surrounding parishes who annually take mandatory Hunter Education classes.

LDWF officials predict the center to be completed and ready for public use within a year.

The Department already provides an education facility at the Alexander State Forest Environmental Education Center in Woodworth near Alexandria. Construction and staffing was funded entirely by P-R. This very popular site provides classes and training for citizens of central Louisiana. It includes a rifle range, shotgun range, dormitory and classroom and provides a permanent location for additional Department instruction, as well as for public recreation.

LDWF's Wildlife Division receives the bulk of the state's P-R allotment, which this year amounts to more than $1.6 million. Approximately two-thirds is devoted to the million-plus acres of the wildlife management area system, including development and maintenance, research and data collection. Most of the wma acreage is managed exclusively with P-R funds.

The rest of the Wildlife Division's share is divided among various research and management programs: deer, waterfowl, forestry, turkey and upland game (woodcock, quail, pheasant).

Although sportsmen fund Pittman-Robertson, they are actually a minority among beneficiaries of the program. Roughly 70 percent of visitors using lands managed with P-R funds are not hunting. They are fishing, camping, bird watching, taking pictures, hiking or otherwise enjoying the outdoors.

Most of the country's animals are non-game species, and these creatures have also benefitted greatly from the protection and management of habitat.

Additional funding goes to LDWF's Ecological Studies section to investigate impacts on the environment by construction projects like water-control devices, and to administrative costs.

"Nobody likes paying extra taxes," said Dave Morrison, Louisiana's P-R coordinator, "but everyone can see the benefits. Enhancing the quality of wildlife habitat and providing enjoyable outdoor recreation is our goal. That can only mean good news for everyone, hunters and non-hunters alike." ◖

Roughly 70 percent of visitors using lands managed with P-R funds are not hunting. They are fishing, camping, birdwatching, taking pictures, hiking or otherwise enjoying the outdoors.

Photo by Alex Demyan

Villars, Justin C.	Marrero
Walker, Richard D.	Shreveport
Walker, Russell A.	Shreveport
Walker, Steven C.	Shreveport
Wheaton, III, James	Port Barre
Wiggins, Daniel P.	Monroe
Williams, Amy D.	Metairie
Williams, III, Charles	Metairie
Williams, Jr., C.T.	Mandeville
Williams, Susan B.	Mandeville
Adams, Jade M.	Shreveport
Aucoin, Brent A.	Erwinville
Barrilleaux, Brandon	LaRose
Bouquet, Kevin J.	Bourg
Brown, Charles C.	West Monroe
Brown, Charles H.	Arcadia
Bullitt, Michael S.	Colfax
Galloway, Everette	Delhi
Carline, Elizabeth	Morgan City
Cenac, Brent J.	Houma
Cenac, Jr, Christopher	Houma
Chaney, Patrick E.	Baton Rouge
Collara, Steve	Arabi
Dominique, John P.	Thibodaux
Dupre, Jason M.	Chauvin
Finnan, Ryan P.	Metairie
Foote, August L.	Lafayette
Gibbons, Jeremy L.	Sulphur
Gonsoulin, Jon M.	Bourg
Goss, Alexander T.	Baton Rouge
Grouchy, Catherine	Baton Rouge
Higdon, cody M.	Ferriday
Hutchinson, Douglas	Newellton
Killingsworth, Kevin	Bogalusa
Knight, Christopher	Baton Rouge
Leitz, Gordon T.	Slidell
Lincoln, Curt T.	Buras
Lugenbuhl, Justin J.	Napoleonville
McInnis, Jacob C.	Baton Rouge
McLure, IV, Thomas	Alexandria
Milner, Eric W.	Lake Charles
Mineo, jr., Kevin A.	Abita Springs
Noel, Jason O.	Church Point
Noel, Matt D.	Church Point
Parria, Ross A.	Lafitte
Patrick, Lawrence	Bastrop
Piazza, Bryan P.	Baton Rouge
Pinegar, Jr., John	Baton Rouge
Rains, Clint M.	Robeline
Rawls, Benjamin A.	Lake Arthur
Regard, II., Daniel	New Orleans
Toups, James P.	Gray
Turner, Brett L.	Monroe
Walters, Michael A.	Otis
Wilhite, Donny M.	Bossier City
Williams, Daniel J.	Bogalusa
Alleman, Jake D.	Belle Rose
Autin, Stephen J.	Covington
Carson, Cody E.	Youngsville
Demary, III., Elza	Sulphur
Griffin, Charles L.	Donaldsonville
Killingsworth, II, Gary	Tallulah
Lagneaux, Raywood	Carencro
Leininger, Arvis B.	Port Allen
Minsky, Louis R.	Baton Rouge
Petit, Jason M.	Ama
Regard, Andre F.	Franklin
Regard, Jady H.	New Iberia
Robinson, Shannon	Homer
Rycock, Max S.	Lillie
St. Germain, Michael	Metairie
Tolson, Kyle S.	Monroe
Tureau, Steven C.	St. Amant
Williams, Juliet T.	Branch
Wilson, III., Charles	Jackson
Allbritton, Brandon	West Monroe
Alleman, Blake	LaPlace
Arbour, Timothy	Walker
Barber, Brian	Baskin
Beadle, Aaron	Delhi
Beaty, Christopher	Haughton
Bourgeois, Laban	Thibodaux

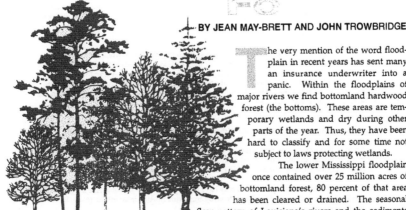

BY JEAN MAY-BRETT AND JOHN TROWBRIDGE

The very mention of the word floodplain in recent years has sent many an insurance underwriter into a panic. Within the floodplains of major rivers we find bottomland hardwood forest (the bottoms). These areas are temporary wetlands and dry during other parts of the year. Thus, they have been hard to classify and for some time not subject to laws protecting wetlands.

The lower Mississippi floodplain once contained over 25 million acres of bottomland forest, 80 percent of that area has been cleared or drained. The seasonal flow pattern of Louisiana's rivers and the sediments deposited during the periodic flooding create and maintain floodplains. These areas are natural holding zones. When a river overflows its banks the velocity of the water drops. The water simply spreads out as sheet-flow away from the bank. No longer able to carry its load, the sediment is deposited resulting in the rich loamy soils associated with floodplains. However, if water is retained for long periods of time with little drainage then the more hyrdric soils characteristic of swamps are found. Sediment deposition in floodplains varies due to climate, geological setting, and human factors. The seasonal timing of floods may coincide with high rainfall upstream and that will contribute more sediment. Agricultural activities once allowed a lot of sediment to enter rivers, but modern practices of topsoil conservation have decreased that source. Likewise, the damning and leveeing of rivers for navigation and flood control have altered the sediment load in the rivers.

Bottomland hardwood forest are filled with a rich assortment of plant and animal life. Woody plants grow around the margins of the bottomland itself, and pioneer herbs such as Indian pink and trees such as the tupelo gum and cypress have adjusted to the short term flooding. A wide variety of salamanders (tiger, marbled and southern two-limbed) are neighbors to box turtles, alligators, snakes, and crayfish. The temporary pools of water are breeding places for many amphibian groups. Fish species include the gar and bowfin (choupique). Large mammals such as the threatened black bear favor bottomland hardwood forest.

Loss of bottomland hardwood forest has been extensive. Much of this reduction has been conversion of the land to agriculture. Other sources of conversion include tree farming monoculture and urban expansion. Taken together these factors have resulted in the serious destruction of a valuable habitat resource. In 1979 through judicial action bottomland hardwood forest were considered to be a wetland and subject to regulations per Section 404 of the Clean Water Act. The Clean Water Act is now up for reauthorization and once again these areas may be threatened by political agendas.

There are major differences in bottomland forests depending on the elevation zones and season changes. If you have an opportunity to do so, try to take trips into this area at different times of the year. Take your camera, binoculars, and sketch pad and periodically return to the locations and make comparisons.

Sight: In the spring look for the flowers such as irises to be in bloom, while the palmettos show their flower clusters in the fall. The flowers of trees such as dogwoods are quickly noticed, but the less conspicuous flowers of other tree species often go unobserved. Above the palmetto plants notice where light comes in from the forest canopy. As you walk from the low areas to the ridges, notice the change in species. See if you can define zones based on differences in vegetation you observed. Also look for the debris line that illustrates the path of high water currents when water rushes through the forest during the wet season.

Smell: At times the air will be filled with the odor of rotting earth and decomposition.

Sound: If your visit is in the spring, you may hear the light-rain sound of caterpillars dropping. In the fall the air will be filled with the sounds of wasps and buzzing bees. A chorus of frogs will entertain you during evening excursions into the forest.

Taste: During a late spring visit, you may have the opportunity to try some ripe mayapples, while a fall trip may provide a chance to enjoy some vine ripened muscadines. (Note: Be sure of your identification.)

Touch: Collect seeds along the trail as you walk. How are they dispersed? Do they flutter, sail, or drop straight down? Test your guess by throwing them up and following their path. Open the seed up and examine the treasure within. Touch a palmetto leaf, notice its fan-shaped blade, and trace the main vein up to the point. Close your eyes and try to describe the bark of different types of trees based upon touch.

Activity: Make a Leaf Collection

- Collect leaves from your forest trip or even from your yard and neighborhood.
- Make that part of your souvenir collecting when you take trips (cheaper than a tee-shirt).
- Try to collect leaves in the fall when they change colors such as the red leaves of the maple and the yellow leaves of the gum. In our families, we both recall using encyclopedias to press and dry our leaves.
- You can make a simple plant press out of plywood, cardboard, newspaper, wax paper, and a couple of long bolts (4 1/2").
- Cut your plywood into standard paper size (8 1/2" x 11") rectangles.
- Place two pieces together and drill a whole the size of your bolt mid-way along the top and bottom edge (the short sides).
- Cut pieces of cardboard the same size.
- Place leaves or flowers between a layer of wax paper, newspaper and cardboard.
- Tighten down the bolts with slight pressure.
- Store in a dry space for a couple of weeks.
- Mount your specimens on card stock and place in vinyl sheet protectors. You can then make a notebook of your leaf collection.
- You may want to organize your collection by type of leaf or by location from where it was collected. You may put pictures of the plant next to your specimen. Whatever you choose, enjoy your nature hobby.

Behind the Badge

BY MAJ. KEITH LACAZE

Get Caught Doing It Right

The summer boating season is here again. One of the advertisements encouraging boating, and doubtless the sale of boating equipment says, "There are two kinds of people, those who are boaters and those who haven't tried it yet." Probably not entirely true, but on a summer Saturday afternoon at the local lake it looks like everybody is trying it.

For wildlife enforcement officers boating safety is a major responsibility requiring more training, time and equipment each year. Water patrol duty demands constant awareness, skillful boat operation, complete knowledge of boating laws, keen powers of observation and the ability to handle people with courtesy and diplomacy.

The duty can be a challenge and the problems can start the moment you arrive at the dock. Complaints ranging from littering to swamping to property damage commonly greet an agent. These abuses can cause over regulation and closure of environmentally sensitive and privately owned areas.

Common sense and respect for others are things no law can create, yet they are the goals we seek when making and enforcing laws. Good conduct on the water should be considered part of planning and preparation for a day in the boat. Here are some suggestions on ways to make life easier on everybody at the lake. Not only can we do it, we can ask others to do it too.

Respect for others begins at the boat launch. Park vehicles and boat trailers in designated parking areas to avoid blocking ramp access. It is surprising how often public launches are blocked by improperly parked equipment.

When underway, consider other people's safety and comfort. High speed passes can be both annoying and dangerous. Swimmers, skiers, fishermen and slow moving boats should be avoided whenever possible. When it is necessary to move past fishermen or anchored vessels, reduce speed to idle. It is the right thing to do for courtesy and safety considerations. High speed also produces wakes which can damage shorelines, docks and other boats.

Boaters must also respect the rights of shoreline property owners. Property rights extend to the water's edge and may vary with the current water level. The privilege and freedom to navigate the water does not include the right to use the land. Always obtain permission from the owner before launching or mooring on private property.

Keeping the noise down, especially around waterfront homes, is a courtesy homeowners and others on shore greatly appreciate. Engine noise, radios and the human voice carry a long way over water.

One of the most prevalent problems on the water today is littering. Although prohibited by law, illegal waste disposal is a constant environmental embarrassment all over Louisiana. The amount of litter found along the shores of our lakes and streams is surpassed only by the variety of containers, packaging material and food products of which it consists.

Litter is an eyesore and a threat to wildlife. Carry a litter bag onboard and use it. Nearly all boat ramps provide waste disposal containers. Bag your trash and dispose of it properly.

Ethical boating means good manners, courtesy and compliance with the boating laws. As boating law enforcers, wildlife agents come in contact with a great many boaters. Our primary concern is safety on the water. We strive to achieve a safe environment by removing alcohol or drug impaired operators from the water and by enforcing navigational rules. We ask to see safety equipment and inspect it for serviceability. It is our job to see that the proper precautions are taken to avoid accidents and injuries and protect lives.

The greatest pleasure of the day on the water is inspecting a well maintained boat, piloted by a competent operator who has all the required safety gear, including life vests which properly fit the wearers. One who is making sure he and his passengers are using the gear. That boat owner/operator is doing it right and got caught doing it right, which is far better than just getting caught.

As part of our effort to keep the waters safe and to educate young boaters this summer, wildlife agents will be carrying something on patrol in addition to the citation book. It is something we think is far more preferable than a citation and a lot more fun to give.

Starting in June, wildlife agents on boating safety patrol will hand out t-shirts to children we see wearing a life vests aboard a vessel. The t-shirts will be part of our "Get Caught Doing It Right" campaign to educate boaters and encourage the use of personal flotation devices (life vests).

Laws and regulations protect lives, property and our natural resources. Common sense, good judgement and courtesy cannot be legislated. Treat other boaters the way you would like to be treated, do it right and have lots of fun on the water this summer.

Sgt. Mike Drude and son Cody show the t-shirt that enforcement agents will be giving to children who wear life jackets.

Teaming with Wildlife Initiative Endorsed

Recognizing that many Louisiana residents are eager to take part in outdoor recreational opportunities unrelated to hunting and fishing, the Louisiana Wildlife and Fisheries Commission officially endorsed wildlife diversity funding initiative "Teaming with Wildlife" at its regular March 6 meeting.

"Teaming With Wildlife" acknowledges the growing number of people interested in hiking, camping, bird watching, canoeing and just enjoying and preserving the state's wildlife resources.

The initiative calls for federal legislation to provide funding for these activities through a user-pay concept of a modest surcharge on outdoor products, such as birdseed, canoes, camping equipment and backpacks.

The Teaming with Wildlife initiative will enable LDWF to expand outdoor opportunities that it can offer Louisiana citizens. With some thought and planning, and very little cost, it can ensure a future for species like tree frogs, cardinals, bats, butterflies and other critters that are common today but may not be tomorrow.

User-generated fees on non-game recreational equipment could generate $350 million a year or more for state wildlife agencies, earmarked for the remaining 95 percent of species that are not hunted, fished or trapped.

For more information contact: Gary Lester, Louisiana Department of Wildlife and Fisheries, 504/765-2823, or International Association of Fish and Wildlife Agencies, 444 North Capital Street, N.W., Suite 544, Washington, D.C. 20001; 202/624-7890.

Teacher Workshop Successful

Fifteen educators from around the state took to the field recently for the first Louisiana Teacher Outdoor Workshop, held Feb. 28-March 2 at the Department of Wildlife and Fisheries Environmental Education Center in Woodworth.

The weekend seminar was designed to expose teachers to outdoor, hands-on environmental education topics in an interesting and memorable way. It is hoped that they in turn will use this experience to excite and ignite the interest of their students to the wonder of the great outdoors, the wetlands, and its preservation.

Sponsored by LDWF and Ducks Unlimited, with donations from Miller, Friends of the Field, the event was free of charge and incorporated a variety of activities to teach the teachers. Representatives of grades K-12 participated.

The seminar was so well received that another is planned for September. For more information on the Louisiana Teacher Outdoor Workshop, contact Bud Carpenter at 318/487-5882.

Wildlife and Fisheries Web Site Up And Running

You can visit the Department of Wildlife and Fisheries on the Internet at *www.wlf.state.la.us* for information about the state wildlife agency.

An extensive set of maps and information on wildlife management areas is available for viewing now. Things proposed include maps and points of interest of all wmas, refuges, scenic rivers, artificial reefs and selected waterbodies, all fishing and hunting regulations, job information, species information, games for children and families, Louisiana Conservationist magazine subscription information and sale items, and speedy correspondence with LDWF administrators and biologists.

E-mail webmaster Coles at coles_cc@wlf.state.la.us.

1997-98 Wild Louisiana Stamp Art Selected

The painting of Baton Rouge artist and architect John J. Desmond has been selected to adorn the 1997-98 Wild Louisiana Stamp.

The winning artwork is an exquisite illustration of cypress trees in a Louisiana swamp.

Desmond, a Louisiana native, received a bachelor's degree in architecture from Tulane University and a master's degree in architecture from M.I.T. During his 40-plus years as an architect he has received more than 25 national, regional, state and other design awards for his building designs. He is the author of *Louisiana's Antebellum Architecture* and the 1994 recipient of the Baton Rouge Art Council's Mayor-President's Award for 'Excellence in the Arts."

The 1997-98 stamp will go on sale July 1, 1997, at parish sheriff's offices, LDWF headquarters in Baton Rouge (2000 Quail Drive), LDWF's New Orleans office (1600 Canal Street) and stores statewide. Prints will be available for sale from the artist. For more information, call 504/387-3381.

Correction

In the March/April issue the information on the 1996 Wild Louisiana Stamp, the fritillary butterfly, was incomplete. To obtain more information on where to purchase a print, write to Rosemary John, 947 Louray Dr., Baton Rouge, LA., 70808 or call 504/769-4727.

Fishing Week Declared

June 2-8 has been declared "Fishing Week" in Louisiana in recognition of the estimated 898,000 anglers in the state. Louisiana Fishing Week coincides with National Fishing Week.

For the weekend of June 7-8, a recreational fishing license will not be required to fish in Louisiana waters.

Paul Jackson, LDWF Aquatic Education Coordinator, stated, "Fishing is a sport that anyone of any age can enjoy. One of the purposes of Fishing Week is to introduce young people to the sport and to give families the chance to enjoy some quality time together."

Sport fishing provides recreation for more than 60 million Americans. It generates in excess of one billion dollars into Louisiana's economy annually through spending on equipment, transportation, lodging and other expenditures. Money paid for licenses, taxes and fees provides funding for federal and state programs that contribute significantly to the preservation and protection of our natural environment.

Looking for the First *Louisiana Conservationist*

LCM staff are still in search of the first issue of *Louisiana Conservationist* (then titled *Louisiana Conservation News*) dated January 1923. If anyone has information on where to obtain a copy, write to Louisiana Conservationist, call Marianne Marsh, Editor, P.O. Box 98000, Baton Rouge, LA 70898 or call 504/765-2496.

Louisiana Conservationist Helps Find Kids

Missing: Jacqueline Annette "Jackie" Beard. DOB: 4/16/87. Missing from Clarksville, Tenn. Sex: female. Race: white. Height: 4'7".Weight: 55 lbs. Hair: sandy. Eyes: hazel. Child has freckles and a scar under her chin.

Anyone knowing the whereabouts of this child should call the Montgomery County Sheriff's Office at 615/648-0611 or the National Center for Missing and Exploited Children at 800/843 5678.

Reminder

The July/August issue of the *Louisiana Conservationist* magazine will be in standard format instead of the traditional calendar. The calendar which is usually produced as the July/August issue has been moved to the January/February 1998 issue. The new calendar will run from January through December 1998.

Couvillion Appointed LDWF Undersecretary

Gov. Mike Foster appointed Ronald G. Couvillion Undersecretary for the Department of Wildlife and Fisheries.

Couvillion will oversee operations of the Department's Office of Management and Finance and is responsible for accounting and budget control, contract management, grants management, program analysis and management, personnel management, data processing, procurement and general administrative services.

He previously served as Assistant Secretary and then as Undersecretary for the Louisiana Department of Economic Development. LDWF Secretary Jimmy Jenkins recommended Couvillion for the job to Gov. Foster. "Given his history and background, especially his familiarity with the entire budget process, his appointment will really be a plus for us," said Jenkins. "We're happy to have him on board."

Correction

The photo credit listed on page eight of our March/April issue was incorrect. The picture was taken by Leo Quebedeaux of Eunice. We apologize for this oversight.

STATEMENT OF OWNERSHIP, MANAGEMENT AND CIRCULATION
(Required by 39 U.S.C. 3685)
1. Publication title: Louisiana Conservationist
2. Publication No.: 246778
3. Filing date: 1/31/97
4. Issue frequency: bi-monthly
5. No. of issues published annually: 6
6. Annual subscription rate: $10
7. Complete mailing address of known office of publication: 2000 Quail Dr., Baton Rouge, LA 70808
8. Complete mailing address of headquarters of general business office of publisher: 2000 Quail Dr., Baton Rouge, LA 70808
9. Full names and complete mailing addresses of publisher, editor and managing editor:
Publisher, Louisiana Department of Wildlife and Fisheries, 2000 Quail Dr., Baton Rouge, LA 70808; Editor, Marianne Marsh, 2000 Quail Dr., Baton Rouge, LA 70808; Managing Editor, Maurice Cockerham, 2000 Quail Dr., Baton Rouge, LA 70808.
10. Owner: Louisiana Department of Wildlife and Fisheries (nonprofit) 2000 Quail Dr., Baton Rouge, LA 70808; mailing address, P.O. Box 98000, Baton Rouge, LA 70898; no stockholders.
11. Known bondholders, mortgagees and other security holders owning or holding 1 percent or more of total amount of bonds, mortgages or other securities: none.
12. For completion by nonprofit organizations authorized to mail at special rates. The purpose pose, function and nonprofit status of this organization and the exempt status for federal income tax purposes: has not changed during the preceding 12 months.
13. Publication name: Louisiana Conservationist
14. Issue date for circulation data below: 3/1/97
15. Extent and nature of circulation:
Average number copies each issue during preceding 12 months:
A. Total no. copies (net press run): 40,000
B. Paid and/or requested circulation:
1.sales through dealers and carrier, street vendors and counter sales (not mailed):none
2. Paid or requested mail subscriptions (include advertisers proof copies/exchange copies): 39,000
C. Total paid and/or requested circulation (sum of 15b(1) and 15b(2)): 39,000
D. Free distribution by mail (samples, complimentary and other free): none
E. Free distribution outside the mail (carriers or other means): none
F. Total free distribution (sum of 15d and 15e):none
G. Total distribution (sum of 15c and 15f): 39,000
H. Copies not distributed:
1. office use, leftovers, spoiled 1,000
2. return from news agents none
I. Total (sum of 15g, 15h(1) and 15h(2) 40,000
Percent paid and/or requested circulation: 100
Actual no. copies of single issue published nearest to filing date.
A. Total no. copies (net press run): 40,000
B. Paid and/or requested circulation:
1.sales through dealers and carrier, street vendors and counter sales (not mailed): none
2. Paid or requested mail subscriptions (include advertisers proof copies/exchange copies): 39,000
C. Total paid and/or requested circulation (sum of 15b(1) and 15b(2): 39,000
D. Free distribution by mail (samples, complimentary and other free): none
E. Free distribution outside the mail (carriers or other means): none
F. Total free distribution (sum of 15d and 15e):none
G. Total distribution (sum of 15c and 15f): 39,000
H. Copies not distributed:
1. office use, leftovers, spoiled 1,000
2. return from news agents none
I. Total (sum of 15g, 15h(1) and 15h(2) 40,000
Percent paid and/or requested circulation: 100
16. This statement of ownership will be printed in the May/June 1997 issue of this publication.
17. Signature and title of editor: Marianne Marsh Editor
I certify that all information furnished on this form is true and complete. I understand that anyone who furnishes false or misleading information on this form or who omits material or information requested on the form may be subject to criminal sanctions (including fines and imprisonment) and/or civil sanctions (including multiple damages and civil penalties).

How to Boil Seafood

In addition to boiling water, preparing good boiled seafood requires the correct blending of seasonings as well as preparation and cooking time. Whether it's crawfish, shrimp or crabs, the following ingredients will ensure consistently flavorful seafood.

Combine the following ingredients:

- 5 gallons of water
- 3 finely chopped onions
- 1 whole peeled garlic
- 3 thinly-sliced lemons
- 1/2 cup chopped celery
- 6 bay leaves
- 1 bottle liquid crab boil
- salt to taste

To make peeling easier, add a little oil or oleo to seafood while boiling.

Bayou Shrimp Casserole

- 2 cups cooked rice
- 1 small package. Velveeta cheese
- 2 packages cooked chopped broccoli, onions & garlic sauteed in butter
- 2 cans Cream of Shrimp soup (season to taste)
- 1 pound boiled shrimp (peeled)

Saute the seasoning in butter. Heat the cheese and soup in a sauce pan. Be careful with the cheese as it burns easily. When the cheese is melted add the seasoning and mix well. Add the shrimp to the cheese and soup. Add the rice and drained broccoli to the soup and cheese and mix well. Sprinkle bread crumbs on the top and place in the oven for a few minutes to thicken. Mushrooms may be added.

Bayou Scampi

- 8 dozen crawfish tails
- 1 tablespoon nutmeg
- 1 cup light rum
- 6 garlic cloves
- 4 sticks cinnamon
- olive oil

Saute crawfish in olive oil. Add spices and steep for 30 minutes. Remove spices and pour heated rum over crawfish. Serve on slices of toasted French bread. Serves 4.

Oysters Mosca

Drain oysters overnight in a colander in the refrigerator. Coat a flat baking pan with olive oil and then add a little more olive oil. Place oysters closely together in pan.

Sprinkle heavily with seasoned bread crumbs including liberal amounts of Italian cheese and garlic. Sprinkle lightly with olive oil. Heat in 375 degree oven for 30 to 45 minutes. Time will vary with pan size. Oysters should be slightly brown and moist but not soupy. Additional bread crumbs can be added while cooking if necessary.

Recipes and photograph taken from <u>The Official Louisiana Seafood and Wild Game Cookbook</u> .

Lightning Source UK Ltd.
Milton Keynes UK
UKHW020217030119
334668UK00005B/178/P